WANTING IT

WANTING IT

Diana Whitney

Harbor Mountain Press

Harbor Mountain Press, Inc., is a 501(c)(3) organization dedicated to works of high literary merit. Harbor Mountain Press books are distributed by Small Press Distribution, a non-profit organization, through GenPop Books and Distribution, and through our website. The Press appreciates support.

Grateful acknowledgement is made to the editors of the following publications where some of these poems previously appeared. "Grand Canyon," "Work" in *The Crab Orchard Review*; "Outer Heron," "Summer Injury" in *The Examined Life Journal*; "Watched Pot" in *Lyric*; "Blood Orange," Hindsight" in *Puerto Del Sol*.

Special thanks to Sophie Bodnar for producing media projects around the publication of this and other Harbor Mountain Press books.

SERIES EDITOR
Peter Money

LAYOUT
Josh Clark

COVER ART
Julia Jensen
juliajensenstudio.com

Harbor Mountain Press
PO Box 519
Brownsville, VT 05037

www.HarborMountainPress.org

Thank you to Cleopatra Mathis, Cynthia Huntington, and Tom Sleigh, for a strong start and lasting inspiration. To Helena Echlin who kept poetry alive at Oxford. To Tom Andrews, Laura Kasischke, Ellen Bryant Voigt, and Major Jackson, for keen correspondence and close readings. To book shaman Suzanne Kingsbury and all the writers at our Tuesday night Salon, where many of these poems were written. To Andrea Useem who said poetry was a matter of survival. To Chip Livingston, brilliant editor, who helped the book take shape. To the Vermont Studio Center for the gift of four writing residencies. To Syd Lea for kindness, encouragement, and opening doors. To Peter Money, my intrepid publisher, for taking a chance.

A thousand thanks to my parents for everything. And to Tim, Ava, and Carmen Whitney, for bidding me leave to write, and for always welcoming me home.

DW

TABLE OF CONTENTS

I.   WATCHED POT

II.   THE WINTER ROOM

III.   DRINKING THE SNAKE

IV.   CHANNELING

For my mother
and in memory of my father

I. WATCHED POT

PECKERVILLE

I didn't want to shock
the neighborhood, pour my hot
crystals into the ice bleach-blue. Still,

I tried on men like dresses, the lace
to take to the wet smoky dive, or the silk
for Mozart & cheese in the meadow. City mouse,
country mouse, I trapped them all

up here where we eat flowers & lambs,
we eat the birds from the sky. Each weekend

another truck in the drive, gone before Church
but always spied by someone, the oldest
lone farmer in Peckerville, making his rounds

on a homely tractor, his wagon full of young
white cedar brush, cut fresh & steamed open
in his old cedar still, trickled slow
down a rusty pipe & skimmed

for a few precious bottles of oil. Sticky, thick
& black as pitch—when he fired it up,

the whole town smelled like Vapo-rub
or the lubricant
for the barrel of a gun. Blackfly season

shot specks of blood along my arms
& I dug in my nail to get out the poison.

X marked the spot & I stayed put—so what

if the neighbors watched me dance in the glass
or bask in the garden in my cape of red hair— was I

the heroine or the femme fatale? Did they
mistake me for the pin-up girl
posed on the mud flap, the silhouette

tapping the milk tanker's wheels?
One-night stand, two-night stand, everyone

counting, except me in my peignoir
with a vase of thistles, dabbing
more scent on the backs of my knees. I woke

sometimes in a veil of disbelief,
those amazed mornings
after two hours' sleep when you meet your own face

& it looks like a girl's, strangely bright, alert
& lacking remorse. You always think
you're changed but you're not

of course. Once
two hundred men shared this piece of dirt,
worked the Peckerville sawmill
till it turned to ash. Two hundred men,

or maybe twenty, enough
for a legend but not for me,
June the shapeshifter caught leaving the scene.

My black-eyed girls bloomed
all over the fields, my Susans not taking no
for an answer, & the sweet-peas climbed

like pros up the net, tendril by tendril
as I scraped the beds clean. Like a dirge, the cows

lumbered into the yard. They were swinging
heavy, laden with dreams.

The fence was hot. The barn
was waiting. I told them
ladies, there's no way out.

WATCHED POT

At the young farmer's dance party the wife's
Eight months gone, her belly a basketball,
Impossible drum, round & taut
Under an Indian smock, so big it's hard
Not to reach out & touch it.
She's like the great cloud of apple blossom
Wreathing the treetops, too radiant, too much
Life under skin. She sways
In the fairy-lights & I just watch, her eyes
Closed in a private dance, slight shimmy
In her shoulders as her man
Works the sound, jumpy & earnest, spinning
House & trance. Because I can
I throw my body around their floor, shake
My hair until the hot sweat runs. Wake
In the morning like a child without dreams
& slowly remember I belong to no one.
Stand at the stove with my white robe undone,
Waiting for the hot silver pot to boil. Don't tell me
It always takes longer this way— I'm hungry
To catch the first bubble rising.
Then the rolling water receives the eggs
One by one, gently, like a pillow.

HINDSIGHT

It was the kind of night June was made for,
a night worth twice its weight in syrup, lemon balm air
like a soft damp cloth wrung & wrung
by capable hands. It was a thick night you could eat
alive, a souped-up night of steam & ginger,
a night no one quite believed was real
except it was there & ripe for the picking,
cash crop of love under the butter moon.

The boys & girls slipped out of their skins,
took the dark lake like a sidelong glance,
parted the curtains of cedar wood as the firefly
meteor shower began. One boy on the shore
cupped a bug in his hands. It was cold light,
perfectly efficient. He showed it to the girl
dripping oil & water, how the bulb kept pulsing
but gave no heat. The night spread a rumor.

But the girl believed it. Her heart was a peach
in a bowl of bones. His heart was the stone
& he hunted for insects, spelling her name
in fire on the sand. He said *look the moon's
drawing water*. Meaning: forecast. Meaning: rain
though she heard *you are the halo, the weather,
the circle of cirrus conjuring change*. Then the night
stepped out of its black chemise & lay its head

across their laps, the pale night shone
like a coin in a crack & they fell to their knees
to palm it. Night of fingers, night of tips,

shameless night that would not sleep, pastille
night she put under her tongue & sucked the sugar
till sugar was spit. Then he slipped it quickly
into his pocket & it balled up small, picked up
lint. It swallowed its pride & turned to a pebble,

then a piece of gravel, then a speck of grit.

WANTING IT

Wasn't I beautiful, wasn't I desperate,
didn't I give a shit about world peace, inner peace,
only wanting it, wanting it, secret graffiti

spelled out in lip gloss on the locker-room wall?

The new underwire bit into my ribs, pushed
me up and I caught the mirror, wanted it, cocked a hip,
wanted it— front seat, back seat,

down on the floor, brag of bruises
blooming like plums on my neck, tender,
bad and legitimate. I wanted

to ditch it, wanted to drive, alone

in the car for the first time, silence, such
concentration my hands tongued the wheel. I could see
the brush-stroke of each yellow line, could feel

my tires crush pieces of gravel, and my ten toes
alive inside my shoes, firm and quick
on the pedals. There was an orange

lodged underneath the clutch. Squeeze it and shift,
squeeze it and *there*. Those boys

who juiced the halls with slouch
and threw their bodies around the field— they watched
when I punched it to second, third, burned my tracks

along the high school tar. They looked at me
as if I could kill them. They wanted to kill me
back against a locker. I could feel

my body jammed up on metal, my skin
in ridges where the grates dug in,

my skirt hiked up, my muscles like fish,
my third eye watching from the outside in.

I was some other girl.
I was anyone's candy.

GREEN

When I kissed Ralph Tamburro at the sixth grade dance
at the Little Red Schoolhouse, his parachute pants
swishing above high-top Nikes, his black curls shorn
but for a tail hanging down, when Ralph kissed me
in the little girls' room by the miniature sink, not French
kissing yet but five wet, real kisses, boys jumped off desks
and girls preened and whispered and Twisted Sister
screamed *We're not gonna take it anymore.*
I was proud of my feat, like 100 on a spelling test.
I kissed him in the bathroom and later in the yard, kissed him
like a soldier, solitary and brave. I knew Ralph's lips
had branded me *Fast*, making the cool boys circle like sharks
at recess, smirking *how'd you like that tongue sushi at the dance?*

When Ralph asked me out in the blaze of October,
I was playing with my friends in the Girls' Tunnel,
our wrists flanked with rubber bracelets, legs armored
in zippered jeans. Ralph sent his emissaries
from the Boys' Tunnel— three of them appeared
to block out the light, arms crossed and high-tops planted.
They stood there like cops, savoring our fear.
Are you green? the tallest one interrogated me. *What?*
I said, looking down in my lap. *You know, afraid of sex
and stuff like that— Green.* The color hung in the air,
color of grass growing under our bodies, color of summer's
last canopy of leaves, color of the mountains like a bowl
around our town, ancient shore-line of a glacial lake
back when our playground was mud at the bottom.

Three boys guarded the mouth of the tunnel. Like a weapon
they wielded their power to name. *No*
I said scornfully, narrowing my gaze. *No way* I repeated
rolling my eyes. *Will you go out with Ralph?* the tall one
asked, and when I said *OK* they vanished as one
and the sun rushed in like heaven to blind us. *Let's get out of here*
I told my friends. We scrambled the tunnel and sprinted
the field, pounded the blacktop where rubber balls soared
and other girls spiked and tallied their scores. I knew
right then I was over my head. I'd chosen my color, the color
of autumn, maples on fire, apples falling like shells, crates
of Delicious and Jonagolds. I'd chosen my color
forever as red, the opposite of green— not what they said.

BLOOD ORANGE

The night the moon turned to rust
we opened all our doors,
brought strangers to our kitchen
and danced in sheer dresses.
We wanted it to change us, the planet's shadow
moving like a spread of iodine
over white skin, unbearably slow
dulling the clean bright round
till midnight, when it crossed back again.
                              On my tongue
the taste of your lipstick, sweet and metallic:
you made me so beautiful
I couldn't speak all night
and stayed close to the glass so the moon
could touch me, my cheeks cool and matte
with powder, my face a pearl
in the strange light. I couldn't
look at you when you did it,
when your hand drew my mouth
and widened my eyes, black kohl
on the lash-line, scarlet-filled lips.
In the morning his kisses
flowered on your neck like plums,
a little blood coaxed to the surface in whorls,
delicate as fingerprints,
startling as scars.
                    Dazed and unclean
we drank tea in the noon-light
and you lay on the grass
while I peeled an orange,
digging under the hard rind piece by piece
until the fruit was bare in its soft skin.
My fingers opened the shock of crimson,

bright and unreal in the white air;
I put a section in my mouth and felt the color
run everywhere.

MAKING BABIES

When I see Leah & her 6-month belly, she's sweet-
talking her blonde toddler on the Post Office floor, his hands
around her ankles as he chants his mantra, *big poop, big poop*,
words like two bubbles blown & popped, two pebbles
he keeps plopping into the calm pool
of adult-recycled air, its murmur & restraint. Her belly
sits proud in the tight bib of her overalls. She pulls her boy
off the floor & lets him lick her stamps & what I notice
are her flip-flops, her white narrow feet, pressing down hard
on thin rubber pads. The color of that skin is close
to violet. It's the color of my morning glories finally blooming
now the days are cool & the apples flushed, pale trumpets
serenading the reckless gardens, showing off
before the frost, more delicate than lacewings, thinner
than rice paper but not afraid of what's to come, a cold
like cold fire that will blacken everything, rise up
from the earth & fall down from the sky & overnight
sear the grass at its roots. Leah's twenty-five. She wears
her gold hair in a knot pierced with a pin. I watch
her pale feet descend the Post Office steps, pad over the cross-walk
into the Laundromat. This is her real life.
This is her day I know nothing about. One baby, two babies,
three babies by winter, & I'm falling farther behind
without even trying, all the women I know shacked up
& glowing, their men stoic & farming or pounding nails,
raising barns, splitting wood, growing food,
making babies. That's what people do here, sooner or later.
The dream's alive & kicking on the Post Office floor. I run
through a river of moss & cedar— the balsam gets into my blood
through my breath. Last night I swallowed a whole white moth,

it just flew down my throat & I couldn't
cough it up. I tasted the feathery lump
at dinner, felt a ghost dissolving in my body's acid bath
& now it's part of me, worked into my cells. Leah says
she knows her baby's a girl. She says they knew
even before they made her. One night her man said *I feel a girl spirit,*
let's make a girl baby, & although it wasn't a plan, or even practical,
how could she refuse? This time of year you horde
what you can. You run your errands & make the rounds,
garden to stove to freezer to garden, as the thumb-sized hummer
zooms up to the glories, buzzing like a loud & dangerous bee,
sticks its needle into a fluted trumpet
& darts back to safety, some nest in some tree. Everything
wants sustenance, no matter how small. Everything's
hungry for the last nectar. If I had babies
I'd be fattening them now, buttering sweet corn & salting tomatoes,
ripe hearts bursting on the windowsills while the dark
comes to dinner, presses against the glass
like some outcast wanting in, some prodigal relation, a face
unacknowledged as I turn my back, put out the light
to make it disappear. I slip under the quilt
the way I check for the mail,
trusting there's nothing in there.

GRAND CANYON

I never knew rock could look so soft,
cliffs bruised with sun, muted reds and pinks,
the mild, exposed colors
of flesh, though sometimes flesh
feels like rock, warm to the touch
but resistant. When he bears down on me
in my desert bed, I think how hard
we both are, how heavy. I can take his pressure
and he mine. This night is a canyon. Slow

as geologic time it forms, from rim to basin
rock bedding down with rock.
Loosed after too much wine
his flat hands move my hips, our bones shift
deep beneath the skin, roll and grind
in calcium sockets, the pelvic flare
and ribcage kiss, knee pinning knee and hips
jammed together, plates of our foreheads—
two forces, one substance.

I think I've gotten the myth
wrong again. In another poem
there would be water—rain on the window
or the faucet leaking. When I remember
the Navajo story, it's the woman
who is liquid. She trickles through cracks and ledges,
works down to the inner gorge
drop by drop, small seep at the contact
of deep red shale with underlying slate.
She is creek and spring, damp earth, dark bubbling,
a haven for mosses clinging to wet walls.
She leaves prints of ancient rains
spattered across the talus slopes, she feeds catclaw

and desert almond, seep willow
and arrowweed. In the basin she roils
brown and wild between rock walls, unleashed
like a freight train, roaring froth and swirl.

And if he is limestone, siltstone,
the sandstone that will crumble in a hand,
slab after soft slab, she cuts through him. This was the creation.
Two forces locked in one empty landscape,
plateau rising up, river bearing down, water and rock caught
in an embrace so fierce, it wore
a gaping hole into the earth.

THE MAINE DREAMS

"All blood should be saved."

—*How to Stay Alive in the Woods*

1.

A fish in the hand is an electrical charge,
wet life twitching for water.
I couldn't kill it.

A fish feels nothing like skin.

I gave it to my brother and he clubbed it hard: once, twice on the top
of the skull, then a glazed quiet
in the bottom of our boat. It's summer,

the girls are learning they're beautiful.

My lazy-eyed sister, sixteen and golden,
my dark cousin with her bra made of string—they wear chokers
of shells, white shells like teeth

and old flannel shirts unbuttoned and frayed—
faded blue of the lake at dusk,
faded green of the island in rain.

They understand the shirts only make them more lovely.
They know how the razor irritates the skin, chafe
and burn at the delicate leg crease, as they oil themselves
and braid themselves, and on the boathouse deck they murmur

and paint, the harsh smell of acetone
rising from their toes. It's summer,

my mother is fishing from the dock. She arcs the rod
back over her head, whips
the invisible line to the rock pile, and reels

slowly, watching the water, her silver-blue
rapala swimming unfinned.

Rustle of the stashed sail
rolled around the mast. Rustle of the wind-sock, hush
of the deciduous. Half the long morning

we're drunk with sleep. Black tea with milk,
milky tea with sugar, we stagger the cabin until the dreams disperse,
so many, so vivid, like feathers or milkweed,

silk floating behind our eyes.
If we try to trap them
they drift away, spinning. Sleep

is a fish in Maine, it swims
all night in the cabin's dark,

in a lake made of blankets, an underground room, all of us
in our deep private drowning

before we wake and gasp, rinse off our faces, and I peel
the curling scroll from the white birch
and write it all down again.

2.

It's summer,

I'm learning distress. The signals

come in threes: three fires in a line,
three puffs of smoke, three gunshots in a row. My book
says don't go to the woods without a coil of good rope
and a mirror to sweep the horizon—

still, we stay alive here. My mother, barefoot in the boat,
steps on a lure, the three barbs deep
in her white heel. She kneels on the seat

attached to the rod, *don't move, don't move,*
my father barks, and she breathes steady as he works it out
with pliers still smelling of fish. He is quick

and careful like my brother with the bass,
how he holds its wet upper lip
to paralyze it,
or grips its middle with one hand to calm it

if the barbs are in deep, or fouled in the gills.

It's summer and I just want to sleep.
Wild chives in the rocks, white-caps on the lake.

My one fish fought hard but it was barely a keeper.
My father brought back the pink and white meat,
the silver-tinged filets in a piece of wax paper,

and she breaded them in cornmeal
and the butter sang
until the fish was six bites
on a paper plate, and we thanked it and ate it and wished

for more.

3.

The girls want sugar and carbon, they want noodles
and cheese and salt. They take the phone
in the closet and lock the door.

If you need to, you can catch a fish with bare hands.

If you don't have a line, you can unravel your sweater,
hide a piece of bone in a gob of bait.

If you don't have a lure, you can use a button.
Sometimes a fish will even close its mouth
on a strip of bright cloth in the water.

                                        It's summer,

my sister's belly is bronze, her navel flashes
an amethyst ring. Spaghetti straps, flip-flops, glitter—

she brushes her hair till it crackles static
as I watch her in the mirror
from behind my book, a swathe of low-back
exposed above her jeans. *Stay*

on your guard, I want to say, my mouth
opening, shutting again. Air rushes like water
down my empty throat. I don't know yet

how to warn her about anything.

4.

The cabin roof is talking
trash, the island a sponge, soaking up rain,

the lake a sinkhole, bottomless, green.

A sunken birch sways deep in the channel,
some white arm that shouldn't be there

haunting me as I swim above it— fear and the shudder
of life in dark water—

and I close my eyes and crawl faster for shore. My mother
stands in her suit on the dock, coiling her hair

into her royal blue cap. My father swims in a trance
to the Big Rock. My brothers

fish and the fish are biting, they swim
down deep when they see the boat, they jump
and tail-walk, they throw the lures, and the lines

go slack, disappointed. Waves slap rocks,
socked in from the South. Without clocks
we wake drenched and reeling

from sleep. Everyone we've ever known
appears in our dreams, frame after frame

until the lights come up
and we peel our lids open again.

5.

It shouldn't be this hard
to kill a fish. When I hold it

against the floor of the boat, it twists
right out of my hands, lashing. My brother

takes over. My brother has practice. A fish is alive,
a fish is dead, just a thing
in bilge and rainwater, black-green and floating

with the baler and sponge.
Get your life jackets on, my father tells the girls
and they buckle up tight over pastel bikinis,

grab the end of the rope with their white fists
and he chokes the engine and rips at the cord

and pulls them flat-out behind the boat while they hang
on the inner tube, screaming, golden
legs whipping out over the wake. They thrash

against the waves and the waves
slap back. They dance the rough surface
until everything's spent. On the deck,

my mother with her hand on her brow,
reeling them in on a thread of worry. White pine watcher,

wolf tree in the wind
as cedars play the lake on their skins, sun
on water moving light over wood.

If you have to, whittle a stick at one end.
Carry a torch of flaming birch-bark
to spot fish in the dark and spear them.

6.

My sister leaves in the middle of the night.

I'm dreaming of cakes, a banquet of cakes,
tortes and layers and buttercream poison
at the wedding of someone I used to love

and I wake to her bed, empty
and rumpled like a face after dreams.

The girls left first, drove home
for a party. Now the trees seep light after so much rain, too long
on the island and I might never leave— wild mint

in the rocks, the hawks tracing spirals, invisible
paths of my risen dreams. And here

are the true and false, the veiled ones, here
are the death caps, the allies and earth-tongues.
Everything breathes here, before it's killed.

It's summer, and even the mushrooms have gills.

II. THE WINTER ROOM

BEFORE THE KILLING FROST

It was too much to ask.
The weeds stopped growing.
And September's tangle was free

for the taking— yellow fist apples
blackberry thumbs, wild ginger
glazing the cedar woods. Yes

everything promised
had come to pass. Even the burning bush
turned crimson. And we lay down

on the creeping thyme bed
under the sunflower roof.

Dark red pansy. Darker beet.

The tomatoes' green glass
refusing to blush.
I took down the ladder

took down my hair, dug holes
for the tulip bulbs
shedding gold skin.   Planted

those hard white tears
in their skins.
Last harvest.

The sudden geese
parting the air. My life

rushing past me again.

DIVINING

The big winters come in threes,
& so we are due.

Summer died last night. I was driving

fast down Cemetery Road—

my high-beams carved a white tunnel through the black,
swept the edge of the corn
with their x-ray fury, the corn

flashing by like a bamboo forest, so huge & leafy
I didn't recognize it.

Home. No porch light:

forty degrees & dropping fast.

The gardens were uncovered & the coyotes
whooped it up, the cat out hunting, the dog out cold
but trembling now & then, whining in her sleep—

what kind of dreams will bring a dog to weep?

I wanted to be the kind of woman
who always has a bag packed, a small bag
with underwear & potions
ready for the road at any moment.

I planned to follow my life
like a divining rod, & where it dipped
I'd stop for awhile. Dig for water, drink.

How could I know that a stick would root me

here, at the crossroads of dust & corn,
here in the boreal forest of change, the winter

coming on like a freight train roaring,
pulling its rattling months of cold?
And me on the dark road, parallel to the tracks,

racing that engine to the river.

HOOF & MOUTH

Not the water hemlock, white root
like a parsnip, tempting sheep
in swamps & thickets,

not baneberry on its thick red
stalk, cluster of shiny china
doll's eyes, each with its one
black dot,

not adder's tongue,
not devil's bit,
but something on the wind, alive
in old water, in pastures, straw
in blankets & sheets—

a cow just breathes it in, poor girl,
& so it begins, the way lust
takes a body, shoots it clean
& builds it a pyre:

railway sleepers, timber, straw,
then coal, more straw, more wood
& coal. Burning all day,
all night, the darkness
molten above a fortress wall,

molten above a woman in stocks,
her forehead pressed to the oiled board,
molten above a sick man's bed,
the wicks gasping

in livid cups, his back
slicked down like flesh
in the sauna, as I pour more water
on electric rocks

to draw all that is poison
clean to the surface.

ON BARR HILL

But I ran it again, there were voices—
maybe hunters in the sugarbush, faint & alarmed,
calling behind me

like the geese on the day they leave,
talking a gray skein over the sky.

I ran it as the sun sank at 4:15, a ball
of pink yarn disappearing in trees,
black branches knitting that light into pitch, the blanket
of winter descending.

Up here you can run for hours alone.
You can criss-cross the woods & never

meet a soul. I flushed a ruffed grouse
& the sudden winged panic
beat its blind way through the brush & my chest. In the air,
wood-smoke, a sweet smell of snow—

first snow, the snow that smells like no other,
when the ground isn't frozen but trying
to freeze, vast heaviness, stillness,
the clean buzzing glow, the smell of someone

who's come in from the cold
when you're in the warm kitchen covered in flour
& you put your arms around their coat
& breathe.

This isn't the end, the end already came.

This is the start & I ran it again,
the cold hill under my body yielding,
the last cord of wood I stacked by porch-light

still heavy in my limbs, the wet
chunks of blow-down,
hurricane wood from two years back
bought from the oldest bachelor in town, the one
who talks from the side of his mouth
& holds a conversation with a woman's

feet. *You remember that hurricane?* he asks them
& they do—it blew
all the kitchen windows in. These things happen

even in Peckerville, even far from the sea
in a valley of cows, something barrels through
& kills the power, floods the rivers, fells the trees.

On Barr Hill the first snow hissed like steam,
relentless sound from another century,
when the mountains were bald
& sheep ate the landscape
down to bare rock, to scar & moon,

when the hill farms were abandoned
& the kerosene burned
& men harvested ice
in blocks & slabs. Always the snow

comes before ice, & I ran in it slow
without expectation. When I rounded the corner
& came upon two fires,

the smoke I'd been smelling for miles
alone, I wasn't surprised,

though no one kept watch. The big piles
popped & spat in the snow, live coals
smoldered like lava under ash, barbed wire

twisting black out of those heaps, & no one
was there to witness the burning—

except me, & I fled back down.

BLIZZARD

Look how the big snow moves up the coast
spilling road salt over its shoulders, weeping without a sound.

Look how it obliterates the windows, the women
drawing curtains across black glass, their men stroking them
with one hand, absently, the children trapped
in bright gymnasiums, the dog pack
hunting souls in the alley behind the school.

Soon the sidewalks will be tunnels and the meters standing stones.
Soon the houses will be ice caps,
big snow inside my mother's kitchen,
her red rice, black vinegar, spring water and wine.
Big snow diluting her Yorkshire tea, clouding the mirror
as she pats cream on her lids. Snow in her scalp
as she mists her pillow with sleep,
summoning her dream of 1969, live at the Apollo
when she saw the King of Soul, dancing in her love and hate beads,
spinning like the storm center over Cape Cod,
white swirl on a radar screen.

You could trace her back through years of weather,
the girl she was, her hands full of fish.
You could follow her north to the Hudson Bay,
let her run her course, a night, a day, stalled out
against the high pressure wall, cheek to the permanent cold.

Look how she offers her face to the tide.
Look how the high tide swallows the blizzard.

And she steps to the deck of a waiting houseboat
and coils the ropes and shrugs the bow free
into the current of a manmade river,
bound for a landlocked sea.

FIRST SUPER BOWL AT MY HOUSE

Dark snow-road to the General Store, is it down
in single digits again, wheel so cold I steer with two fingers,
banks so high my car bounces right off them
back to the middle of the road and drives.
Parked outside, in a running minivan, a woman sits hunched
over a box of pizza, cradling a slice in both her hands
as two kids in car-seats scarf down their pie, a family so hungry
they can't make it home. I came for milk and a block of cheese.
Whole milk, not skim, thick as saliva, sating the winter
craving for fat. In the dusty aisles, a man's on my mind,
he came from the West with his heart in a pack,
his Grecian body riddled with scars, a story I invented
in a summer of longing but the story took flesh
and the flesh arrived. Now I'm buying him bags of salt
and ice, I'm bowing my head to the arctic air.
The woman in her van doesn't want to go home,
maybe nobody's there, or worse than nobody, so she sits
in the dark when the pizza's gone, when the kids fall asleep
and the store shuts down, she watches the gas needle
slowly drop—half-tank, quarter-tank, eighth and drive.

At my house he cranks like the furnace on high.
He rises like the sun and shines all over, talking of the time
he dressed in leather, walked the red carpet at a Hollywood party,
said he was a rock star and they all believed him, who wouldn't
believe he was a god or a king, some power source burning
inside the body that scares my hand when I graze his skin
and forces water from his pores, his eyes. Sometimes
he slides like hot butter into milk. Sometimes he's a warrior
in ripped blue-jeans. On-screen the heroes in silver helmets,
thighs like pistons in silver tights, beat hard on each other till
one breaks free, runs for safety, runs for his life.

On my couch he swipes chips in sour cream, sits braced
up high between hope and fear. I drink his aura
like strong dark beer, amazed like Alice growing smaller
and smaller, *go baby go baby*, my chin on his knee.
On a good day he's like Pedro Martinez, walking to the mound
with a rocket in his sleeve. And the mound is already halfway
to the plate, he stares down the world, he gives it the heat.

I'm the girl in the bleachers tucked in a peacoat, sitting
on my hands in the early season. The crowd like a sine wave
rises and falls, the scent of pizza floats from the halls, and I know
how she feels, the minivan woman, alone with her bundled-up,
red-faced hunger, an engine running that's not her own
though it keeps her warm, its gets her home. I don't know
football but I know weather. I know ice, like water, flows
and travels. There are sheets of ice a hundred thousand years old,
two miles thick, moving over the poles, actual glaciers
on their way south, where we sit in the dark with fat in our mouths
as the magic clock starts and stops and starts
and girls in silver boots kick the floodlights out.

CABIN FEVER

It gets better, it gets worse again:
lace & slush, gray on white. I heard February arrive
on snowmachine, whining through the night

with her Cyclops eye, leading a wild train
of 2-stroke engines, pistons firing
to eat up the forest, forty-five, fifty,

fuming like warriors, teeth bared & helmets low
as they circled the house then revved in the yard,
vowing to make me pay. But what did I do?
I only wanted green. On the warm side

of a cold front, the snow turned blue
at 5 o'clock, the air stripped naked & shivered
in the spruce boughs, the spin cycle shook
the whole basement clean. I swear

I thought I could make it till April,
but the depression out back
where the chimney smoke settles, that lowland

where spinach lies under the snow,
keeps filling with smoke that won't drift or disperse,
that creeps all day down the roof's sleek pitch

& hangs like a terrible thought
by the window.

WORK

When cold bloomed like lichen on the windowpanes
and the wildflower honey hardened in its tub,
when we found ice each morning in the bedside water-glass,
when the pipes froze too and the landlord
arrived with a hair-dryer to blast them, we knew
the winter was testing us. Too tense to sleep,
we took to the wood-pile, working in silence in bitter air
till our arms burned and faces ached, heaving the logs
down the chute to the storeroom, taking pleasure
in one motion repeated— cold wood cradled

then thrown. This was the good work, felt
and measurable, transfer of matter from one pile to another.
If we couldn't talk to each other or sit still
at our desks, poems eluding our fingers like wraiths,
words escaping like warm air along windows, at least
we kept the heat source. The monster stove yawned all night
and we fed her. We tended her belly
with the utmost care, raked the live coals and disposed
of the ashes. Without gloves or tongs we offered log
after log, our skilled hands darting in and out like sparrows,
brave against the blinding heat. Slaves to fire,
we guarded our time: January, February, her hunger,
our work, the clean undisputed refrain. And when the thaw came,
we recalled our desire, its indistinct duties,
and learned how to speak it again.

THE WINTER ROOM

> *You're a damn fool if you stay*
> *But there's no better place to go.*
>
> *—Gordon Bok*

1.

When the last sun burns through double pane glass,
sets fire to the old blue canning jars,
olive oil turned to molten gold, clover honey to amber,
molasses to tar, even dry white beans made relics
or runes, piled like molars from a small god's jaw,
I feed the demon
in the firebox, ply that genie with tinder and meat,
let him lick the bark then wrap it whole,
rage wild beneath his soot-black kettle
filled with cloves and cinnamon, singing

Nothing you wanted means anything now
Whatever you lost will never be found
Everything known is here in this room

and the dusk will come in a minute or two
then ink-blue dark, then the end of blue
and if I choose I can sit all night inside it
and breathe that invisible jungle.

2.

Go back a century,
nothing is sealed.

This house stands on bare ground.
Frost seeps up through the floor.

Wind slips through each cedar clapboard,
through plaster, horsehair, lyme—no difference
between the air outside
and air in here

until the family seals off the stairs,
shuts the inner doors,
hangs blankets over rimey windows and lives
together in the winter room.

Fifteen cords.
They don't speak to each other any less
or more.

The oldest girl hoards
a square of good dark chocolate,
the one boy sleeps with his hands
between his knees,

the blizzard begins
that will fall all winter
and five thousand miles to the east

my ancestors scavenge
for frozen potato seeds.

3.

My fear? That the coals will be dead
                                in the morning, ash,
silt and char, start over. That flint
won't shine, rock maple won't burn.

That one coal will jump like a finger
unseen, smolder the floorboards
until the house takes that tinder,
eats itself alive.

Without it, I'm nothing.
Without it, my life begins.

4.

Ten degrees deep in the heart of winter
I'm driving twilight on the edge of too fast
as a snow dervish whirls in the hard blue field

and swords and daggers jut from the eaves
pulling a cold front across the Arctic,
air sucked all the way from Siberia

pure as vodka, thin as salt, rasping my throat
with iron and frost. A girl can't stand it,
all this beauty—

it makes her want to scream or hold
perfectly still, a birch branch poised
above each lacy track, each rodent claw

and snowshoe drag. January
takes me like a shotglass, neat, a bite
of some clear liquid flame. Suddenly

I don't go out anymore, don't want to go far,
there'll always be dancing, always Saturday night
but never enough winter, never the sun

like a coal on the hills, that last shocked
streak of rose burning snow,
the white round bales more white than snow.

If I start to slide I'll ride the skid
let the car go
past the buried sugar, past the farm

where the great tanker idles in wait,
the cooling milk pumped slow from the barn
into the shuddering silver tank,

milk roiling up those sleek curved walls
like fuel into the belly of a jet.

5.

Never get used to anything,
not Peckerville, jade plant, orange pekoe,
not your body buried under quilts alone,

not two hundred pounds of deep wet snow
rumbling the pitch like thunder.

You could walk out a door
and be crushed in an instant.

You could dream of a cream
silk strapless gown. Someone could ask
you to give this up:

your weather, your stories, this town.

6.

I know about cupboard love
but still I love waking
to cats milling my ankles,
the hungry dog wagging
her whole body for me,
waiting for hours

as the deer browse cedar
and the ice sinks a layer
under their steps.

My mother,
queen of cupboards,
knew the dogs loved her best.

Once she threw a whole gallon
of milk at my father—
it just bounced off his chest
and gulped out on the floor.

Sour smell of ingratitude,
then the dogs' eager tongues
lapping the linoleum to death.

Love is that hungry.

Love eats recognition.

7.

My fear?

That I'm broth, clear ochre,
or swinging like the onions
in their wire cradle—

that the room keeps me safe
and boils me down, makes me an offer
of soup-bone, ash.

That I'll never leave here.
That I'll leave.

III. DRINKING THE SNAKE

JANUARY THAW

Red sky glows like hot metal
above the black mountain. Out of the inky dawn
comes a warning: new moon, prophesy of change,
something buried beginning again.

Who lit the match?
The tinder's within us.
A hundred and one channels of the heart

and your hands are still traveling my spine
at the speed of a sentence. Is it fever
or the memory of fever? January thaw

glistens mud-slick roads and I find new tracks
in wet snow, hoof-prints and boot-prints,
the hunter and the hunted. All night
silent creatures circumnavigate the mountain,

one following the other following the other
in a trance of survival. Cut the grapevine
for a drop of water. Chew the birch-bark

for wintergreen. I dreamed the red tattoos
covered my belly and thighs, pale skin painted scarlet
as if the cells burned within

while the sunken firebox
smoldered beneath the snow, buried
under layers of leaf litter and humus,

forged long ago out of transmuted
hunger, and I dug and dug like a fox
for a taste of iron.

PRE-NUPTIAL

I've been making soup all winter
from the sack of potatoes sprouting eyes in the cellar,
wood-scrap and stove-ash, dried sage

and a hunk of ice I hacked off the roof.
Six months up here the lakes are frozen. A body
carries winter in her shoulders, the accumulated weight

of January's clothes hunched against the wind,
digging out the car again,
tromping around with fifteen pounds of wool.

When you don't touch me I assume I'm not
beautiful. My wedding gown hangs like a ghost
in the guest room, bust stuffed with tissue,

winking with beads, champagne silks floating
on the cold draft breeze. I move it to the shower rod
when I take a bath, hoping the steam will smooth

out the creases, but in its luminous presence
I can't relax. *Let him guide your spine,*
the dance teacher says. *He is the puppet-master,*

you are the puppet. But I'm also the witch
with my pot of winter, breaking in the golden
wedding shoes. The soft leather gives as I feed

my two fires, traipse in high-heels for armloads
of wood, murmur spells into the simmering stew.
Still I don't know which story to use, which

of the only two tales in the world:

A stranger comes to town, a man goes on a journey.
Or a woman, of course, it might be a woman

clad in furs in a snow-blind field,
she breaks a straight track for the vanishing point.

A MARRIAGE STORY

Kindergarten was wood-chips and Julio
on my tail like a rocket through the playground,
black eyes and fast legs crawling in the tire tunnel,
breath on my turtleneck scrabbling the rope wall,
bouncing me off the hanging walkway
into the monkey-bar house. Every recess
he said he would marry me. He said it
like a threat, like *I'm going to kill you* and I knew
if I ran too slow and he caught me, it was true.
At home my mother brushed my brown hair
like a precious fleece, static crackling
beneath satin ribbon as I cried for my future,
for my new life with Julio. Even after the promises
and parent-teacher conference, after recess
inside and time-outs for Julio, I cried
like the world was ending, which it was, because
Julio proclaimed I would grow up and leave home,
small prophet in corduroys staking his claim
where boys stashed mosses and secret bones, played out
their terrible shouting games. I was fast
but I couldn't out-run them. In another forest
the girl glimpsed the gold, trick apple of love
concealed in underbrush, and she slowed her sprint
to gather it up. The last warrior who raced her
caught her like this, reeled her in like a fish on a line.
At night in the king bed, my yellow ring shines,
bites my sleeping finger sometimes without warning.

DRINKING THE SNAKE

Both mothers buried a bottle of vodka, old charm
for fair wedding weather— but one week to go
the mercury rose, skunks crept out on the washboard roads
& March rained without mercy on the melting land.
Was it bad luck or good omen? They didn't know

but where did the winter wedding go, lake ice
like a flood plain, snow rotten & dirty as old horse hide?
The farmer fired up his sugarhouse & boiled first sap. The bride
shoveled the porch roof with her bare hands, loosened
successive layers of storm, kicked like a bitch

& watched them slide. The groom hauled deadfall
to the bonfire site. All he wanted to do was drive, roaring
mud-ruts in his pick-up with the dog in the back,
nose pricked to the damp South wind, the whiff
of the turning of an unknown tide.

Then the gifts began to arrive— goblets & blankets
& a salmon from Alaska, & a fist-sized package marked
Thai Love Potion, a baby king cobra coiled in a bottle, pickled
in liquor & yellow rice wine. You drank it for virility,
for lust & faith. When he put it to her lips

it tasted like a snake— salt & scales, the raw burn
of venom. Potent enough to silence the old selves,
flush any doubts from their dark nesting place.
In the full Sap Moon, they fed each other fire
& prayed for what it would take.

GOODBYE MAIDEN

All honey and no moon, another dark wet night
in paradise, drinking mango mai-tais at the Tiki Bar
as fishermen cast fireflies into pounding surf
on the tips of invisible lines. Light draws the *ahi*, the men
arch and reel, the ocean yields— fair is fair. You're sad
as you've ever been here. Silent in the banana grove,
our skin cloaked in jasmine, plumeria, smothered in perfume

dropping from trees. I'm learning to be married too.
Coffee comes from cherries, I never knew—and coral graffiti
is another braille, lovers spelling each other in white pebbles
on black lava by the highway, strange blackboard
of love notes stretching for miles. I wanted to get out
and gather stones for you, but we were exhausted from the flight,
worried about sleep, welcome leis wilted on the rental car seat.

This world's brand new. The island grows beneath our feet
layer by layer, magma plume rising from the earth's mantle,
molten rock breaking through ocean floor.
Can you feel the tremor? I pray for eruption. The goddess
who created this land wants more. All night the lava flows
radiate the day's heat, vents steam along the rift zone
and we cool ourselves in hotel sheets. I dream an old woman

walks the mountain roads, warning strangers of a lake of fire,
cauldron of fire hurling lava in the air, eating the rainforest,
building new shore. We wake to smiles of sliced papaya,
glimpse from our balcony the volcano's cone peak.
Something is about to be born, up there. Someone
is kneeling at the cinder altar. I see a girl on the rim
sacrifice her name, release a trail of sparks into the crater.

FIRST PRIMROSE

All day I dug the garden out from under an iceberg,
chipped away at snow-drift & roof-slide, razed the last bastion
of winter's encampment. Far away, there was a war on.

Even the cats wouldn't stop killing: snakes, moles,
baby field-mice, a big rat, & birds strewn
all over the floors, gray feathers gusting like souls

till I couldn't bear anymore bodies. I fastened two
bell collars round their squirming necks, still they dragged death
back from the underworld. They jingled

all night in & out through the cat flap, as lightning bloomed
in the petrified sky like a nuclear bomb
like the ozone raining, like a divine intention

gone terribly wrong—the electric veins of God
getting high, shooting up smack from the power lines
& no one was going to help him recover, no one

would stage a crash intervention, no one had the guts
or the cash or the time, we all watched as he kept on burning.
Next morning it greened up, just like that. A moose

lumbered down from the bare high hills & porcupines
grazed the fresh hayfields, vacuumed the savory dandelion bulbs,
plump heads about to explode

with petals. April, from Latin *aperio*—to open.
I was learning to be a married woman. My angers
passed like the quick spring snows, lace blankets

thrown casually over new grass. Beneath the iceberg
I uncovered the infant primrose, green fingers
feeling up out of a hole.

PEARL

What luck— to love a man who notices cows,
who feels tender for the velvety Jerseys
& calls every day from his car to the pasture
hey girls, lookin' good—cruising them, meaning it.
Such pretty, thick, black lashes. He knows in a glance
if they're heifers or milkers, if their bags are full,
if their tails are clipped. And what of the white bull
dozing in their midst? He's the one she watches,

fat pearl in the grass, muscles twitching
beneath the sheen of his hide. If he is the god
doomed to be sacrificed, the chosen one
led through the streets on a rope, beholden
by women who long to conceive, stroking his haunches,
meeting his eyes— will he show himself to her
before summer is over, will he claim a beloved,
will he burn, will he rise?

COWRY

Something else was sacred: not me, not my body.
The bone coral clinked underfoot on the bone beach,
remains of the living reef eaten day & night,
feast of fans, feast of blue light. Do fish ever sleep?

Don't touch anything, my mother said, twice,
opening her book of poisonous things:
spines, thorns, shells full of claws. Underwater:
silence, then faint tinkling, a wall of glass

scraped to bits with an ice-pick, the parrot-fish
rasping its teeth on brain coral. It never
stopped, whether or not we put on the masks,
suctioned the rubber to our stinging cheeks

& dropped below the surface to listen.
I took the bone-path to the chain-link fence,
stumbled alone along piles of sea-bones,
some shaped like hands, some like feet,

some without shape beaten smooth by the sea
& shells full of wind like empty houses, as I slipped
like a reed through the cut in the fence & glimpsed
wild goats like gods in the sea-grapes,

their old beards twisted with milkbush & rocket,
their hooves digging code in the sand. *Go back.* Go back
to the sun drowning quick in the harbor, to the family
asleep on balcony chairs. Go back to the banquet

laid on the veranda, the plates cleared in silence,
in silence refilled. The party boats lit up
their strands of pearls, yachts named for dreams
& myths & girls: *Amnesia, Ambrosia, Lolita, Infinity.*

Why didn't I sail right out of the channel,
into the mouth of the open sea?
I was wrong, this island was never a reef—
this island was a flooded, defunct volcano.

In the souvenir shop lay the pick
of the beach, a giant cowry polished to gleaming,
its wet living thing scoured out with gasoline.

GONE

I know nothing about oceans. I learned the desert in a week.

When spring comes to Peckerville, you can watch the grass turn green,
That line of new color moving up the fields. In an hour
The birch trees burst into bud, their apple-skin lace

Frothing against black hemlock. Stubborn sun but it doesn't rain
& one whole hillside shivers dry
Dun-colored grass in the wind. *Don't start any fires,*

My neighbor says. *Ninety-nine years ago this week this town*
Burned to the ground.   Hot wind in dead grass
Moves fast as a thought— one spark, one twig,
One scrap of flaming cedar in the air

& we're gone, the whole dirt crossroads, all ten houses,
Hay fields raging like an oil spill—this town
Flattened & resurrected once a century. I say I wasn't

Going to light anything but I saw them
Burning on the Creek Road, men dousing debris
With rainbow gas, their mounds of dead leaves smoking & licking
      & then I was gone

In my cloud of dust a quarter-mile long. No
I'm not burning, I'm thinking of water— a drip
From the gooseneck faucet, a spray-bottle for the drooping

Pansies, the leggy seedlings in their plastic trays.
In the desert my brother & I found a spring on a mountaintop,
Climbed the Weeping Rock & the Devil's Garden,

Walked Coyote Gulch deep in the canyon where golden
Shiners flashed in the stream, catclaws drooped
& cheatgrass pricked our ankles. We shook out our shoes

For scorpions, knowing what to expect from such a landscape,
No mercy, nests of baby rattlers, wildflowers surviving on fog & dew,
Rosemallow & ghost flower blooming in the rare shade

Making pollen we walked through, blinked & swallowed.
All we had to do was collect cold moving water,
Filter it with ash, keep walking to the canyon mouth
            & turn back. Each night

We laughed till we fell asleep, under breathable mesh & the massive lip
of a red-rock amphitheatre dome. It was bone quiet down there.
It was a cut in the earth. If a fault line trembled

The slabs might fall, & if it was me buried in sandstone
I could bear it, but not him. Back home in Peckerville
it's the biggest winter in decades. Dirty ice & snow

Lodge in cold hollows, cap the high hills until May—
May!— till the thaw comes & the rivers go mad, swelling the banks,
Tearing down saplings, raging brown, unforgiving & thick as soup

& a boy I know takes out his kayak to ride the white-water
            with two friends.
Now they say he wasn't experienced, but he was young & strong
& a friend of my brother. The waterfall pulled him

In his red spinning boat, his yellow helmet poised at the edge
Like a sunspot, a blink, too slow & too fast, the boat at the glassy lip,
            then gone.

The others raced ashore & ran downstream, but he was nowhere,

He didn't come out. Even the paramedics
Couldn't retrieve him, they saw the colors inside the waterfall
But couldn't risk the boom & smash, the angry river

Still rising fast, faster each night, each day. Two weeks
& he's still inside. Maybe he found some
Redemption in there, roared by a thousand pounds of snowmelt,

Encased in a room of hard white spray, thunder in his ears,
Legs tucked in his boat, torso free to recline on rocks,
Did I say he was a friend of my brother? May

Is the month of dredging the lakes, the month they pull up
A man in his ice skates, also a man with white fists still clenched
To the grips of his Arctic Cat. With enough time

Everything comes back, even the green we forget all winter.
Even the rain that pounds the grass, & the village that rose
From char & cinder. Once in the desert my brother left,

Climbed up slick-rock in rubber sandals, pried himself up
The smooth red cliffs to the crest where I watched his back
Turn to a speck, a sunspot against the flaming horizon
            for so long

I thought he'd vanished into the West, but he came back down to me.

DOE AT DAWN

Autumn settles all accounts:
trading brown for green, tendering less
for more. I travel the tunnel
of gold into rust, tread summer's fallen

canopy rotting on the forest floor, brush
banks of jewelweed, hanging seedpods
full ripe to bursting. They explode at first touch
of thumb & forefinger, one last chance

to scatter their story.
You had no claim on me
as I had no claim on you. July's drama
arced lightning across the dome, wrote epics

& symphonies on lake & sky.
Now it's carcass & wishbone in a cold kitchen
standing alone over a soup of regret, torch sunflowers
pressing last petals against the glass.

Fall mornings are dark as cellars, a scrim of frost
etched over grass. The deer rushed by at dawn
like a phantom, hooves thundering on cut corn
before the shadow passed.

If you wait long enough, intensity fades—
the snake crawls out of her used-up skin
& coils in the stone wall. The spiral closes in again,
nestles amidst dry sheaves & stalks.

On another road you too are raking leaves,
stacking logs, reckoning up all we have lost.

OUTER HERON

Summer beckons us with sea glass, hunting
someone's broken trash transformed to gems

for eagle eyes, finders/keepers at low tide.
Playing Hearts, drinking wine, we dropped

into a sunset torpor, slid oysters like cold, salty ardor
quietly into our mouths. You rowed me

in the wooden dory, strong back swinging
a seaman's rhythm, out beyond the Thread of Life
while I perched like a flightless gull in the bow.

Breathe in the effortless scent of Maine—
cedar and moss and money, salt air laced with longing

and white sails scudding, homeward bound.
Wild blackberries nestled down private drives,

a stunning sweep of ocean vista shimmered
just out of sight, beyond the No Trespassing signs.

There was no end to what I wanted,

more than the children snug in their bunks, the foghorn
all night diffusing our dreams, more than white

feather quilts and leather seats, frozen custard flecked
with vanilla bean. So I let you row me
through lazy mist, past Witch Island, past

The Hypocrites, where the Atlantic flowed
clear, cold and pure and I slipped out of myself
into that element, floating like a selkie

above deep green sea lettuce, tresses streaming
like fronds of sea kelp, till the cold salt

penetrated the human marrow and I sobbed
forgive me for my hunger.

IV. CHANNELING

DESHABILLE IN MAY

Thunderstorms beat the pollen from the trees,
swell the river wide as a foreign delta.
I wake to the poppies, half-shattered,
their silks disheveled, fur centers bared
like a woman stepping out of a red dress.

GOD-HUNGER IN APRIL

The long, slow stuttering into spring
gives way like a fist opening, a thunderhead rent,
and sunlight teems in sheets through bare trees.

Barefoot in the garden, I rake dead leaves
off the tips and hints of flowers, the poppies'
furred shoots venturing their course

towards gorgeous excess. Heat radiates
from the stone wall but the high woods
are still buried, ragged snowpack in the cold hollows,

god-hunger in the abandoned sugarbush
where the barred owl calls its rough-throated hoot:
two iambs repeated, insisted, repeated.

I stood there in my blind spot, caught
like a sapling in snow and sun, the green world returning,
the spiral unfurling, the body remembering
its source— *this, this, we live for this,*

god-hunger in the garden caked with dirt and sweat,
soil beneath my fingernails, in the lines of my palms,
dark soil between my toes still damp with snow-melt,

god-hunger in the kitchen in a glass of cold water,
drawn from a channel bored deep into the earth
slaking the first true thirst of the season.

CHANNELING

I told you May was too much, too much.
Knee-deep in buttercups, I run again
to the mountain, beat a path through drenched clover
to the cut in the trees, that quiet arbor
where woods transform into rainforest,
luxuriant air at skin-temperature
though I am almost skinless. I can feel
the canopy photosynthesizing, green cells
drinking light, making sugar. Sweet ferns
unfurl in a spiral from curled packet to lush frond,
striped maple leaves spread wider than a man's palm.
Stinging nettles edge the path beside wild geranium
but I slip past unscathed again
to the summit where hunger surprises me, rising
in a fever of chlorophyll and memory,
your hand on my thigh, your words in my mouth
as I lie back on moss and grass open
to the sky. Hot sun burns through cloud
and light, light, light blooms around my eyes,
a tremor spiraling from deep within the body,
leaving my fingers glazed with honey
that smells of rainwater, leaves, mosses and ocean.

THE GROVE

I'm not the heady sweetness of my mother's peonies
collapsed in a snow of petals on the floor.
I'm the ruffled vein of crimson at the center,
the flower's ecstatic story.

I'm not the girl bowed like a lady-slipper
coyly shading her eyes from the sun.
I'm the pitiless goddess bathing in moonlight
quiver full of silver arrows, keen to deliver
painless death to any mortal who dares
to watch. My body is strung like a bow.

I'm the thunderhead and electrified air,
the poem and the source of the poem.
I am a conduit, a clear channel, a convergence of streams,
the grandmother wolf maple cleaved
at the crest of the hill, the apple tree
hollowed to reveal a tunnel, an aperture
in which you can place your gift: fruit or flower,
jewel or seed.

I'm the hushed fingertip of the purple foxglove,
my speckled throat open to morning rain,
my leaves flushed with toxins to heal a failing heart.
I'm a thousand flaming tongues of honeysuckle
exploding in bloom like a fever dream, falling in a torrent
off the side of the house, solid walls
I abandon in order to pray:

The god carries me into the grove.
He lays me down like an offering
in ferns and leaf litter, cherishes me
with his lips and hands
until my gold skin is flecked with black forest soil.

SIGNS

Not everything is an omen. The wasp nest
under your front porch might not forecast sorrow,
the child's screaming nothing but random consequence,
unlucky marriage of histamine and venom.

Ignore poison ivy gleaming in the hedgerow,
the goutweed choking beds of evening primrose
and Asiatic bittersweet wrapping the old lilac
in the fatal embrace of its suckered vines.

Not everything dangerous is as it appears,
not even the log on the path up the mountain,
damp wood splintered and flies droning
on what you mistake for entrails of a half-eaten

snake. But there is no omen, no dim sorcery
under the oaks, only four baby birds curled
like one mangled creature—featherless, gray-skinned,
eyes closed— a death so strange in the green world

that you leap over and never look back,
running hard straight to the summit, because you can,
because fireflies float each night in the pasture,
flick desire amidst the wild roses,

their bodies emitting cold quick light
like the cursor blinking on your dark screen:
I'm here, I'm here   find me, find me.

SUMMER INJURY

July is fire & thunder
boom & gasp of exploding flowers
high noon blazing above the tiger lilies,
  hay wagon rattling hot bales down my spine.

A little supernova of pain radiates from the base
until I'm willing to give up anything

to make it stop. *What's wrong? what's wrong?*
chirps the mind like a catbird, twitchy & tight
as I drive to the river, pull back my hair,

dive in green water and stroke hand over hand
to the trestle bridge. My shadow moves over murky
bottomland, crosses sandbars, log-jams, sunken trees.

The oak canopy drapes
above me like a curtain, filtering the gold afternoon.

The spine is a ladder you can climb.
The spine is a rope you can pull.
The spine is a strand of white stones in dark velvet

waiting to be stroked, coaxed into submission
but the sacrum is fused, locked like an amulet.

Help me to map the body's interior, the flared wings
of the pelvic bowl. Blindly feel forward, your hands

on the ridges of my hips, grasping for the bones
from the outside in, the calcium roots of things.

BENEDICTION

Open the book of spells again,
distillation of hope and prayer.
Summer is barely a whisper here

passing in successive sheaves of green, leaves
yellowing before your eyes. Queen Anne's lace
froths on tall stems, the dark spot

in the white center like an insect devouring the flower
but when you bend down to look
it's a cluster of bruise-colored petals, a fingerprint

on a wedding gown. Here at the crossroads
of dust and hay, shorn grasses crackle underfoot,
the earth splinters like bone, a red-tailed hawk
keeps screaming above. July

is a metal room that bakes and warps in the heat,
leaves hang wilting on withered trees.
How long? How long until the rain?
Everything you've ever known and loved

is poised in the dry air, shimmers like a mirage
in the haze, refracted in the ochre afternoon—
Open the book. Open the book again.

Remember the love tonic of jasmine and rose oil,
two whole vanilla beans soaked in a cool bath.
Open the book and study the future:

how rain will pour down one night like forgiveness,
how August will pass like a long, torpid dream sequence,
how September will dawn with the benediction of mist,

early morning chill on fall raspberries, pale yellow fruit
hidden on heavy branches, how you will kneel down
in wet grass to pick them

from underneath, slipping the fragrant gems
in your mouth one by one like an offering,
as if you were feeding

the deity inside you: inscrutable goddess
who once scaled mountains

but now bathes in the still river, parting the dark waters
under the swan's eye
of the blue moon.

TOWER CLIMB

Last night the rotten bedroom window
slammed shut and shattered. Glass
broke through pieces of my dream,

peepers throbbed and the long, low train
whistle rose from the river.
You twitched in your sleep but didn't notice

how my heart huddled like a flayed animal
in my chest, bare shards
on the windowsill waiting like weapons.

So I ran helter-skelter past the ice pond, climbed
wet trails up to the tower, half-hidden turret
above the asylum, built by the patients stone

by gray stone. A century ago, they believed
in Work Therapy. Now the gothic tower's sealed
shut—no windows, no visitors, black iron door

locked with two rusty bolts. I circled the base
like a bloodhound, as if something were hidden
in the dark interior, where the Victorian staircase

wound through dust, to the crenellated ramparts
of the rooftop view. Beyond the river, beyond the green valley
the weight of a secret hung in the pines,

mosses clung to black ledge rock, and the train
passed again, calling an old warning,
bearing a message from one elsewhere to another.

TRESPASS

Again I walk out under a waxing moon,
dragging the old dog on her new leash.
In May I was a conduit, a clear channel

now November has me nailed to an empty field
caught between the milkweed and the specks of snow.
You cannot go down the same path twice,

the Professor tells the children when they return
from Narnia. So I scour the dead gardens
with my shears and gloves, tear down

the morning glories from the trellis I made,
ravaged vines light as hay in my arms,
all the skeleton left of summer's

luminous body— blossoms pale
as the underskin of a wrist, blue trumpets
floating like lyrics on a June morning.

My memory—*offer it up*
my hunger— *offer it up*
my pleasure— *offer it up*

until nothing is left but rage, antiseptic
grain alcohol, clear burn in the throat
as I cut back poppies, iris, evening primrose,

turn the scraped beds into scars.
Witness the goddess in her fury
combing the barren woods.

If you've trespassed on what is rightfully hers,
beware her sure aim:
one arrow through your left ventricle,

one arrow through your right palm
pinning you to the rough bark of a wolf maple
your heart flopping like a fish in its bowl of bones,

anticipating her approach—
sandaled feet stalking the desiccated path

while that old moon like a false eye
whispers goat-tongued promises to the night:

You are dark and beautiful,
I cherish you, I need you,
I will never leave you

and the night swallows all of it, starstruck girl,
though she should know better,
though she is left like an empty bed, month after month.

WANDERING WITH THE VICTORIANS

After breakfast I wanted to get lost
on the lowest slopes of Whiteface Mountain
stumbling up someone's lonely sugarbush,
half-looking for the Long Trail.

But you can't get lost with a phone at your hip
hot apple of knowledge humming
connection, chiming *possibility*, a fingertip
stroking for a voice, an answer.

Ducking pipeline and plastic tubing, I trod
on a bronzy carpet of trout lilies, solitary flowers
nodding demurely, gold-haired girls in mottled
skirts, stunned at the sunlight's lack of restraint

and the sudden colonies of white hepatica
identified properly with Petersen's Field Guide,
milky star blossoms shot with lavender
sprung up for a week from beds of winter.

Accuracy matters, in this case,
which is why I dug the wild leek, pried a white shoot
out of damp earth, savored the raw-dirt, allium taste,
and why I won't say I found bloodroot

on the ledges, not even to suggest the grief in my body,
nor hint in the Victorian language of flowers
that bloodroot is a kind of poppy, and poppy
means *imagination*, so whatever stranger's

woods I trespass, you may picture me wandering yours.

OUTER HERON II

Queasy has the sea in it—
our boat rolling & rocking on the swell,
my guts flopping like slow fish

caught on a strand of barbs.
You said, *watch the horizon. A line
doesn't move*— but it did, it did

so you steered to the outermost island & dropped
two anchors into the surging chop,
rowed to the cove of dark spruce,

white rock, helped me walk the cliffs
till the churning stopped & I sat, sleepy,
watching the seaweed. Rockweed

floated in cold salt water, easy, easy
loose & washing. It flowed like hair
in formidable waves, refused to fight,

let go, gave in. Why not
be the arrow pointing to CHANGE,
the barometer poised between FAIR & RAIN?

Even the air here smells of migration.
Even the channel bell clangs us a warning—
changing, changing, changed.

GEESE-GOING MOON

How do we survive this every year,
the damp cusp of winter coming on,
Demeter's grief in a frieze of branches?

I carried the light box up from the basement,
scoured the kitchen with forced fluorescence,
white walls screaming *happy happy*
while the heart-wick sputtered and snuffed out.

In the dark barn the barred owl
huddled deep in her cage, obsidian eyes
in muff of gray down. Acrid
birdshit, sweet hay, I couldn't tear my gaze
from her. She's got one broken wing,
she won't be released.

*

Maybe the moon doesn't mean anything,
just a space rock in orbit emitting
no light of its own, reflecting only
a smudge of the sun that strikes it—
smear of lamp oil in a hazy sky.

Every way I try to render you is wrong,
pulling the thread of language through the eye
of winter, cinching it tight, stitching up the season.

First the spell then the counter-spell
pierced the veil of daily life, dissolved
the known boundaries. My heart unraveled

like tapestry, blood-colored cloth
laid out on the floor. Undone,
I hid the scraps in a chest
and locked the door.

*

A hundred geese in a shaved cornfield
fuel their passage to another realm.

One cardinal caught in wild-rose briars, scarlet daub
on monochrome. And we're still here

scanning the roadsides, reading the full moon, bracing
for the long haul.